NETWORK

TO GET

WORK

Winning Job Search Strategies

for the Reluctant Networker

Alan Jones

NETWORK TO GET WORK

Also by this author:

'Winning At Interview'
'How To Negotiate Your Salary'

ISBN: 978 - 1479380138

Cover design: www.creative-bytes.co.uk

Cover image: © Rodolpho Clix 1 Dreamstime.com

CONTENTS

Introduction

Chapter 5 - Stage 3 - Tell Them There's A War On

Stopping The Lights From Going Out

Lining Up Your Referees

Allowing For The Slow Burn

The 'Thank You And Goodbye' E-mail

Learning From The Experience Of Others

Tracking People Down

Keep A Smile On Your Face And A Spring In Your Step

Chapter 6 - Stage 4 - Give Them The Ammunition

Accept All Information Gracefully

The Follow-Up Email

Have The Self-Discipline To Lose Control

Travel First Class - It Gets Results

Chapter 7 - Using The Information

Handling Referrals

Handling Leads

Turning Cold Leads Into Hot Opportunities

Identifying Your Target Executive

Getting Live Leads From Dead Ends

Laying The Groundwork For A Second Approach

Conclusion

INTRODUCTION

Job-hunting is a serious business but if it were a game it might be described as follows:

'This is a game for any number of players. The game is divided into two halves: the first half is called Action; the second half is called Interview. All players will begin the first half but not all will be playing in the second half. The object of the game is to win the job offer and there can only be one winner. In the first half of the game, players must overcome certain hazards designed to prevent them from competing in the second half. Typical Action hazards are 'too old', 'lacks experience', 'job hopper' and 'poor networker'. Players who overcome these hazards are declared winners and they go on to play Interview. Further hazards are encountered at Interview including 'no enthusiasm', 'talks too much', 'talks too little', 'lacks confidence' and 'unprepared'. At the end of the game the player who has overcome the hazards is declared the winner and wins the job offer. All remaining players, who had previously been winners, are now losers. This is not a team game.'

Now, what makes this game so interesting is that few people can play both halves of the game equally well. One player may be a star turn at **Action** but a consummate duffer at **Interview**. Conversely, another player might play a great game of **Interview** but won't get the chance to prove it until the **Action** hazards can be overcome. But what is it that separates the winners from the losers? The eventual winner of the game is not necessarily the best person for the job. That person most likely got eliminated in the first half. No, the winner of the game will always be the player who has played the game the best. That's why an awful lot of good people get rejected and a lot of awful people get hired.

As with all games there are rules. In 'Winning at Interview' you can learn the rules of how to play well in the second half. 'Network to Get Work' deals with the one element of **Action** which poses the most problems for the majority of job hunters; how to involve your personal contacts in your campaign so that they may help you get work. It's a sensitive issue and you must proceed with caution. If you've just lost your job and feel totally comfortable with the idea of networking then you won't need this book, but you may need therapy. For sure, job hunting can be worrying, stressful and a chore. But it can and should be exhilarating, challenging and enjoyable.

Before we play the networking game, a word about luck. Chance can be a crucial element of most games and never more so than in networking - luck and coincidence have a major role to play, but by their nature you cannot legislate for them. You can however create the conditions under which luck and coincidence can manifest themselves, and this book shows you how to make that happen. You can't trust to luck alone as it isn't a substitute for hard work, but the harder you network the more opportunities you'll get. Have fun with your networking.

---------◆ ◆ ◆ ---------

CHAPTER 1

How To Lose Friends And Alienate People

A job search is an exercise in communication and when yours comes to a successful conclusion you don't want any emotional baggage to carry around. It's essential that you're able to look back on everything you did or said and feel at ease with yourself. You must neither demean nor compromise yourself or others. Your reputation, integrity and self-respect are too precious to be squandered in pursuit of your goal. A small minority of my job hunting clients tell me they are totally comfortable with networking and have no hesitation in ringing people up and asking for help. Yet they are the very ones who, through rampaging around like that bull in the china shop, end up carrying the baggage, losing friends and making enemies without realising it. If you understand intellectually the importance and advantages of networking but baulk at the very idea of actually doing it then take heart because not only are you in good company but you'll proceed with the necessary degree of caution.

When giving advice on networking it's all too easy to say 'Ring 'em all up and get on with it, they won't think any the less of you - feel the fear and do it anyway'. Heck no. For sure, you'll be warmly received and given real succour by some but others think unemployment is an infectious disease and will head for the hills when they see you coming. Now, you might take the view ' Hey, I don't care if they remove my name from their invites - they weren't friends worth having.' The flaw in that argument is that they are often the very people who would have been helpful if only you'd gone about it in the right way.

The Perils Of Enthusiastic Networking

To categorise human beings as 'extrovert' or 'introvert' in the context of a job search can be simplistic and not very helpful. Better perhaps to speak of 'enthusiastic' networkers who often mess up and 'reluctant' networkers who would get it right if only they had a plan. Yes, enthusiastic networkers are not always good networkers and reluctant networkers can be great at it if they have a strategy - and 'Network To Get Work' will give you that strategy. Let's consider some of the personality traits and characteristics of typical enthusiastic networkers:

11

- Often gregarious, outgoing and sociable. With the right balance this 'club-ability' can be an asset but too much of this can lead to *over-reliance* on networking as a route to success in the jobs market. Many make the mistake of seeing it as the *only* route. They kick up a lot of dust, sashaying from one networking event to the other, being wined and dined by their silver haired mover and shaker friends who promise much but fail to deliver. After six months of that they finally realise that responding to job ads, using recruitment firms and making direct approaches is not just for the 'little people' after all. They often end up feeling chastened by the whole networking experience.

- Enthusiastic networkers are often good communicators but forget that listening is a supreme communication skill. As we shall see, networking is primarily about the gathering of information not the giving of it. The gregarious, outgoing type can be too 'me' centric. You know these people. They are the ones who in effect say 'Well, that's quite enough about me. Let's talk about you. What do you think of me?' They have no fear of dominating a meeting and they forget that as long as you are talking you are not learning anything.

- Reluctant networkers are quite rightly protective of their contacts but enthusiastic networkers are not and expect others to be the same. They expect you to just 'hand 'em over' because they are quite happy to hand over a list of all their contacts to someone else. Your contacts are precious to you and there are only so many favours you can call in from any one person.

- Those who have a real enthusiasm for 'working the room' can be short on etiquette and easily disrespect the person they are engaging with at any given moment. They are forever looking over your shoulder for someone 'better' to target. For them time spent building rapport is time wasted - the reluctant networker will see it as time wisely invested. A reluctant networker will engage fully with a contact and not disrespect them by sending the signal 'you have not got my full attention'. They will not be staring at their mobile phone when in your company. Knowing how to 'disengage' from a conversation is an art form.

- Enthusiastic networkers are pretty much 'What you see is what you get' and haven't developed the invaluable ability to adapt their manner to suit the manner and personality of their contact. They fall short when it comes to understanding 'nuances' and 'undertows'. Reluctant networkers can do this too of course but they are more likely to be chameleon like - which is a life skill and not just for job hunting.

- Enthusiastic networkers often lack diligence, are poor planners and can be disorganised. They are often victims of their own pro-activity and are pretty much 'full on' all the time. Knowing how and when to take your foot off the gas is a real skill. Reluctant networkers are often more adept at planning, thinking and organising which is perfect for our strategy in the following chapters.

The Advantages Of The Hidden Market

In this jobs market you don't want to be competing with anyone. That's the art of job hunting. Someone once said that 60% of job vacancies never become public knowledge through an advertisement or recruitment firm. Someone else said it was 70%. The maths don't matter much but let's agree on 70% because it sounds better. Now let's not knock that 30% of advertised jobs - they've been given a bad name by career counsellors. You're not going to apply for them? Oh yes you are but don't hold your breath because the silence can be deafening.

As job hunters we could be forgiven for believing that there's a big black hole out there - a repository for all those résumés and CV's that represent the shattered hopes and dreams of all those job hunters who believed in chasing ambulances. These are the same people who delude themselves into believing that recruitment agencies will find them a job, not realizing that recruitment firms are in the business of finding people for jobs, not jobs for people.

No, ambulance chasing is what everyone else does and successful job hunting isn't about doing what everyone else does. It's about being creative and using initiative. It's about understanding that every job ad is a cry for help from a beleaguered employer and a missed opportunity for at least one job hunter. It's about realising that a job ad or agency mandate is not just a problem seeking a solution, but that it's a problem already defined and they are now seeking a person to shoe-horn into that definition. And it's about realising that job ads don't spring up overnight but are preceded by weeks if not months of procrastination by the employer (that's the one who's got the problem). If only they knew that you were available all they'd have to do is call you up for a meeting and save themselves all that time and money. But you're not in their spotlight - you're standing in the shadows with all your competitors scouring the job ads.

Now with networking and making direct approaches, aka 'the hidden jobs market', you will by its very nature travel down many blind alleyways. Most of the actions you take will have a negative result, but when you get it on the button there's a high chance you won't be competing with anyone, plus, neither the 'problem' nor the 'person' has been defined. They are now more likely to make the job fit you as opposed to the other way around. You could end up writing your own job description.

Incidentally, when people achieve a job offer through networking it often carries with it a job title that would never have attracted them if they had seen it advertised.

---------◆ ◆ ◆ ---------

CHAPTER 2
Getting In The Zone

So - What Is A Job?

If you've already read 'Winning at Interview' and 'How to Negotiate Your Salary' you'll know all about the importance of getting yourself 'in the zone' but I'll have to assume you're coming at this afresh so here goes:

The quality of your networking, and your work in the **Action** half of our game as a whole, is determined by two things:

    1. Your mind set

    2. Your strategy and tactics

We'll work on the strategy and tactics later but let's start by ensuring that you're in the right 'mind set'.

Athletes often remark that doing the training is all very well but it won't pay dividends if, on the day of the race and when that gun goes off, they are not 'in the zone'. Networking is exactly the same. Your strategy may be sound but if you're not 'in the zone' it won't pay off and your tactics will go awry. A positive mental attitude is the single most defining feature that separates the winners from the losers of this contest and in a competitive market confidence is King.

To distance yourself from your competitors and get yourself in that spotlight you have to be 'psyched up' just as any athlete or actor. You must reconcile yourself to the idea that you too are giving a performance. Reluctant networkers often struggle to give themselves up to that idea but give yourself up you must.

Your ultimate goal is to get the right job so let's define terms. Take a blank piece of paper; draw a line across the middle and above that line write down your answer to the question **'What Is A Job?'**

Your answer may be a simple sentence or perhaps a list of words. There's no deep analysis required here - just do it.

NOTE: This is the only 'exercise' you have to do - the rest is just an easy read. But it's important so don't skip it.

Does your answer include any of these?

    'It's a pay check'

    'It's what I do for a living'

    'It's a way of filling my time'

    'It's a means to an end'

    'It's something I enjoy'

    'It gives me status'

    'It allows me to interact socially'

    'It's a career stepping stone'

If so then you're not 'in the zone' and are unlikely to network well. That may be what a job is *to you* but that wasn't the question. The one thing they have in common is that they are all 'me, me, me'. If you look more objectively at the question the true answer may be more apparent and the mist may lift. Now, move out of the 'job hunting zone' and put your 'recruiter's hat' on your head. So in effect you are, just for a moment, the recruiter and the person who has this 'job' to award. Below the line write your answer to the same question 'What is a job?'

If your answer comes close to 'a job is a means of fulfilling a need profitably' (or 'cost effectively' if you are targeting the 'not for profit' sector) then we have the truth and you are in the zone.

We now have two very different answers to the same question that clearly reveal the relationship between you, the people with the power to award you the prize and your network contacts. It is fundamentally a 'seller' 'buyer' relationship. You have something to sell (and you must have clarity about what you are selling) that buyers need and they are willing to pay cash for it. It's a business transaction. No more, no less. There was a time when we liked to believe it was a bit cosier than that, but that was in the days when we thought organizations existed solely for the purpose of employing people.

That no one *wants* to hire us is initially somewhat worrying, but it's nothing personal - they don't want to hire anyone else either. Not for nothing do we call it the 'jobs market'. It's a market place like any other and like any other seller you don't wait for that market to come to you in the form of a job ad. You have to take on the traditional role of 'seller' and take what you are selling to the market. That's what sellers do. The jobs market is the only market where we seem to *expect* buyers to advertise that they need something. It's nonsense. It's also true that, as with any other market, not everyone, or indeed anyone, will want to buy everything, or indeed anything, you are selling at any given moment. That's not necessarily a bad reflection on you or your 'product'. That's just the way it is. And that's why successful job hunting is 97% 'rejection'. Now if you were getting 97% rejection you might start to think you were doing something wrong, but no, if you applied for 100 jobs and got 3 offers that's a great result surely?

If you were running a market stall you wouldn't burst into tears every time a potential customer passed by without buying anything. As a buyer how many times have you walked out of a shop without making a purchase? The seller you have turned your back on has to remain upbeat about it and not take it personally.

And yet, as sellers in a competitive market place we're often psychologically on the back foot because the buyer also has something *we* need - the job - and boy, do we need it bad, and the greater our need the worse our performance. Problems arise then because each party is working from a different agenda. The employer is seeking to find someone to fill a particular role, which is not always clearly defined, and the prospective employee is seeking to find a job. This dichotomy, where each party is dancing to a different tune, has proven to be the rock upon which many a job search has foundered. This won't do. You'll have no credibility, and get no respect, from buyers or your contacts if you play the game of **Action** dressed in the clothes of a job beggar. You may get some sympathy but recommendations, referrals, information and advice will be thin gruel.

Don't Take Ownership Of The Problem

As we shall discover in later chapters not only do you have to get in the zone but you also have to *stay in it* - a momentary lapse of reason, an unguarded comment or any sign of ambivalence from you and your contacts will drift away like smoke in the wind.

Remaining upbeat in the face of adversity is a real test of character but let's be clear - *no one wants to hear bad news*. You may not have chosen to fight this campaign but fight it you must and enthusiasm is infectious - if you've got it they will catch it. So don't take ownership of the problem. The buyer has the problem - you're the solution. If you've just lost your job then you've also lost all those 'above the line' things that made you who you were. You get them back by staying in the zone, drilling down on the problem below the line and showing an interest in the buyer's needs. It doesn't happen the other way around. Introverts can network just as effectively as extroverts - and sometimes *more* effectively. It's simply a matter of finding the right way *for you.*

Five Reasons Not To Network

It's worth looking at the reasons why so many sellers are reluctant to embrace the concept of networking and make it the keystone of their campaign:

- **I don't know anyone.** This is most likely to mean 'I don't know anyone I can talk to in a senior enough position and who can give me a job.' This is to completely misunderstand the meaning of networking in the context of a job search.

- **I can get a job through my own efforts.** This is most likely to mean 'I don't want my contacts to know I've lost my job so with any luck I'll find something before they find out.' It's one of the great paradoxes of job hunting that at the one time in our lives when we should be shouting from the rooftops that we are available for work we go in the opposite direction and retreat into ourselves. This is a sure sign of not being 'in the zone'. Isolation, not deprivation, is one of the primary causes of long-term unemployment. In the jobs market you can't allow yourself to become a victim of self imposed isolation.

- **I don't want to use my friends to get me a job.** Neither 'in the zone' nor understanding the meaning of networking. It's unlikely that anyone can 'get you a job'. The most anyone can ever do for you is secure a meeting with one of their contacts. It's then up to you. As we shall see, you won't be ringing up friends and asking them if they know anyone who has a vacancy - no baggage remember. And why deprive your friends and acquaintances of the joy of doing you a good turn or returning a favour? Most people have a real empathy and understanding about networking these days. Many are in fear of losing their jobs and there's a degree of self-interest in this. They are intelligent enough to figure out that if they support you now they may need to call in their markers in the not too distant future. Nothing wrong with that either.

- **I don't agree with networking on principle**. It's another paradox that those who take this view will, without even realizing it, network every day when doing their job but get all precious about it when looking for one. It somehow becomes personal and 'beyond the pale'. Maybe it's the word 'networking' that instils fear and trepidation. 'Networking' is only a word to describe the gathering and giving of information and advice. No more, no less. It's interesting that networking in the business arena seems to have a legitimacy not bestowed on the job hunter, probably because the 'product' or 'service' is more clearly divorced from the seller, or because for the seller in the jobs market 'unemployment' still has the whiff of stigma about it.

- **I have contacts but they won't know anything.** Your glass is half empty! As a reluctant networker this is likely to be the biggest hurdle for you to confront and overcome. One way of insuring yourself against surprise and disappointment is to take no action. No action no reaction. It's another paradox that when positive job hunters network they almost *expect* to be disappointed - a positive reaction then comes as a most pleasant surprise. Negative job hunters commit the cardinal sin of predicting the outcome of the action and because they predict a negative result they don't take the action.

A Job Search Can Expand To Fit The Time Available

Not for nothing do we call it a job search *campaign*. Like all campaigns there's an enemy and in this campaign your enemy is *time*. Your ability to manage that time is of critical importance. We've already seen that when we lose a job we lose a lot, including our daily routine - all those 'above the line' things that make us who we are. But we also gain something - freedom. We are liberated, elated even. We now have something we didn't have much of before - time - time in abundance. Well, that can be intoxicating and seductive - like giving whiskey to the Indians.

If you're under no financial pressure then sure, maybe you can afford to take time out, recharge those batteries and catch up on all those things that need doing around the house. But be disciplined about it, as before you know it you'll be stuck in the leafy lane syndrome and unable to extricate yourself. Now this can have a real impact upon your networking strategy.

One of the reasons it's always been easier to get a job while you still have one is because you're likely to be in regular contact with people. It's alarming to discover that once you lose your job you can soon become history in the minds of many - yesterday's news. Taking that sabbatical may be a great idea but consider the impact of this on your network contacts - there may be some who would be easy to contact now but much more tricky, if not impossible, in 6 months time. You should be looking for the right job, not any old job, so for how long can you financially sustain a professional job search campaign? Or, putting it another way, at what point in time would you no longer have the courage to turn down the wrong job? If you've got your finances in order and have figured out that you've got 6 months then be very careful because if you are not disciplined that's exactly how long it will take.

Very rarely do we achieve any more than we set out to achieve and if you set out to achieve an offer within 6 months you're unlikely to get one within 3 months - self-fulfilling prophecies and all that.

Moreover, a job offer in isolation is a dangerous thing because the only choice there is 'take it or leave it' and you'd most likely take it because it really does take a lot of courage to turn an offer down. Now if it's the right job then that's not a problem but what if it is a retrograde career move? A job that maybe you were doing 5 years ago?

Taking a salary cut is not a cardinal sin but you'd better do it with your eyes open as there's a saying in the world of recruitment that *'You're only as good as your last job and you're only as good as your last pay check'*. Stating the obvious maybe but whatever you do next will be in pole position on your résumé/CV for the next time you're in the market. Now there's a gloomy thought but the shelf life of jobs is pretty short these days so act in haste repent at leisure. If you're serious about it then your objective should be to achieve 3 job offers within the same time frame and within 3 months not 6 months. Now that's real choice. You'd have to be unlucky if one of them wasn't the right job and you'd have more leverage to negotiate on the salary. You'd be most unlikely to achieve this without networking, as we'll see in Chapter 4.

----------◆ ◆ ◆ ----------

CHAPTER 3

Stage 1 - Reviewing Your Troops

When thinking about planning a network strategy it's a good idea to maintain our theme of 'the campaign'. We now know that time is the enemy but who are your friends? A job search campaign is one battle you cannot possibly win all by yourself. You have to utilise your troops, who in this context are of course your contacts. Now, as we'll see later, when the action really begins and the bullets start flying some of your troops will be steadfast and true. Others won't be at all helpful, maybe because they can't and that's no bad reflection on them. Some are just plain lazy and can't be bothered. Others just don't get it. Structure your networking campaign into four distinct stages:

1. Reviewing your troops
2. Selecting your 'Special Forces'
3. Telling them there's a war on
4. Sending them some ammunition

This structure serves to emphasise the point that networking someone doesn't have to be over and done with all in one go. Protecting the relationship you have with your contacts and avoiding emotional baggage often necessitates a high degree of care and subtlety.

At Stage 1 you will write down a list of everyone you know or have known. I repeat - *everyone you know or have known*. If enthusiastic networkers make a list at all, and most don't get that far, they only write down the names of people they know well, are happy to call, who they know would be pleased to hear from them and who they think might be helpful. They would also typically be in the same line of business and work in the same geographical area. That's throwing the baby out with the bath water (see *'The Strength Of Weak Ties'*). For those people, unless they are very rich in contacts, the networking strategy, such as it is, often unravels early on in their campaign. Three weeks in and they've run out of ideas. Those who say 'I've done my networking' have almost certainly skipped Stage 1.

Networking is never 'done' - it evolves and grows through the course of a campaign. It's the only part of your campaign that *expands* if you do it right. This structured approach to networking sits well with reluctant networkers who typically much prefer to have a clearly defined process with clear objectives for each stage.

The Virtues Of An Open Mind

If we know what our objective is we are more likely to achieve it as it helps us to focus more clearly. When I ask job hunters what they think they want to get from networking most respond by saying 'I want my contacts to tell me of any leads/ opportunities/ vacancies/ jobs or give me introductions to their contacts'. This is not so. For sure, the more of those that come your way the better but in the first instance what you really want to get from networking is *information. Information is the fuel that drives the job search engine and you cannot function without it.* A job advert is information that should be well received by you if it's put in front of you by a contact, but that's the buyer's problem screaming out at you.

Information can come in different guises and from surprising sources. For example it can come in the form of advice from a contact. Advice which may initially be insignificant in itself but which may ultimately turn out to be quite pivotal - it could maybe swing your campaign in a more fruitful direction.

If you persist in believing that your *primary* objective is to get a 'lead', 'vacancy', 'opportunity', 'job' or 'name' from your contacts then you're not in the zone and when reviewing your troops at Stage 1 you will most likely eliminate contacts that would have turned out to be surprisingly informative.

Avoiding The Judgmental Traps

As it's eyes and ears that get information a neat definition of a potentially useful contact is anyone you know or have known who has a pair of eyes and ears; In short, anyone who has a pulse. Even people who are themselves retired can be useful contacts and great sources of information, indeed, your job search can give them something to do and they might be most grateful to be given the opportunity to make a contribution to your campaign.

It's also true that retired people these days are much more active than in the past and are therefore likely to have acquaintances across a wide cross-section of the community. So, if you start with that broad definition and pursue the information then the

34

leads etc will accrue from that. You must suspend your disbelief at Stage 1 and that takes a degree of self-discipline.

Never more so than in networking do luck and coincidence have such a crucial role to play. By its nature you can't legislate for luck - you can though manage your campaign so that you put yourself in potentially rewarding situations that in turn create that luck.

It's essential that at Stage 1 you don't make judgments about your troops. Don't fall into the following judgmental traps:

- **My contacts are not in my geographical catchment area.** Networking is just like the Internet in that it knows no geographical boundaries. Once you open up a line of communication with someone in another country they may be able to give you advice and information that is not location specific or connect you with someone who *is* in your area.

- **I don't know any/many senior people.** If you're not in the zone and are only seeking leads and referrals then you may well be right. Of course the more contacts you have in senior positions the better, but hierarchy need not dictate the quality of networking - in this campaign the humble foot soldier can be just as effective as the galloping major (see *'The Strength Of Weak Ties'*). For example, junior people can be privy to precious information not divulged and enjoyed by some senior people in the same organization. The old saying that if you want to know what's going on in a company talk to the guy on the door is as true today as it ever was. And incidentally, if you *are* a senior person then don't demur from putting junior people on your Stage 1 list. And some of those may be reluctant to offer up information to you as they may think they are not 'worthy' - so maybe you have to find a way to reach out to them. Chickens come home to roost too - if you were nice to people when you were on your way up the corporate greasy pole then when you meet them on the way down they are more than happy to reciprocate. You reap what you sow.

- **I only met this person once and that was 10 years ago - I can't just give him a call - what would I say?** You've slipped out of the zone again as your thought processes have wandered on to Stage 3. Stage 1 is not the time to be fretting over what might or might not come later on in the campaign. As we shall discover later, you may not have to call that person at all.

- **I don't know where this person is - we've lost touch.** Ditto. We'll see later at Stage 3 how this can often turn out to be a real advantage.
- **I know where this person is and she could be really helpful. I could call her but I really don't want to. We didn't get on too well.** Here you go again. Networking when you're in the jobs market can be a real education and one of the things you learn is who your friends, and acquaintances, *really* are. This can of course be both spiritually uplifting and downright disappointing. Common feedback I get is along the lines of 'I'm surprised that this person has been such a great help because I didn't think she liked me that much - but *this* guy who I've known for twenty years, the one I stood bail for and fed his starving family - nada. I thought he would've stepped up to the plate.' Welcome to the crazy world of job hunting.

- **I can't start networking until I've figured out what job I want.** There is some logic to this as there is truth in the old saying that if you don't know where you're heading you'll most likely end up somewhere else. But in the jobs market that 'somewhere else' can turn out to be a surprisingly pleasant place to be, whereas the place you thought you were heading to might have turned out to be a real poisoned chalice. It's precisely your contacts that can help you find the right role that, as we saw earlier, might not have attracted you if you had seen it advertised. As we'll see later, being too specific about what you are 'seeking' can turn off the tap through which information flows. If you tell your contacts that you're seeking a job as a middle manager in a large retail sector company within a 50 mile radius why would one of them give you information about that unadvertised senior management role in a smaller wholesale company 2 miles from your home that's owned by their cousin? Because you wouldn't be interested in knowing about it that's why.

'Not', 'don't' and 'can't' are common to all of the above and they are also your enemy. This is your inner voice inviting you to settle for inertia and stand on the sidelines wringing your hands. Have no truck with this nonsense.

So, at Stage 1 if a name occurs to you write it down immediately, regardless of whether you know where they are, what they do, whether or not you want to contact them nor how useful you think they might be. It's quite likely that if you do this then the time it takes to write the name down sparks the name of another contact in your mind - someone who perhaps you would never have thought of. It may then be this second person you end up networking and not the first. Stage 1 most certainly requires you to take a great leap of faith. But take it you must, and don't forget to involve your partner/family members in this exercise because they are also your troops - and who do they know? Other people can help you build your network.

'It's not what you know it's who you know' has become a cliché but it's not a full and accurate description of 'networking'. A more complete definition would be to say 'networking is about who you know, who *they* know and *who knows you*. If you are beginning to freak at the idea of writing out this

Stage 1 list then go now to '*The Strength Of Weak Ties*' and get succour from that.

---------◆ ◆ ◆ ---------

CHAPTER 4

Stage 2 - Selecting Your Special Forces

You should by now have a long list of troops but no real organisation so now is the time to consider your strategy. Let's have a look at where your networking sits in relation to your campaign as a whole entity. We know that information is the fuel that drives our job search 'engine' but what is this 'engine'? Depending on whom you believe, the statistics of a job search look something like this: Advertised 15%. Search firms 20%. Networking 40%. Direct or Speculative Approach 25%.

That's 100% of a typical job hunter's market but what does it mean? It means that you only stand a 15% chance of getting an offer by responding to a job ad (any vacancy that becomes public knowledge through an online or hard copy advert, including ads placed by agencies); a 20% chance of getting an offer through an executive search or 'headhunting' firm; a 40% success rate through networking and 25% by making a good, well targeted independent approach by letter (and we're not talking 'job begging' letters here - see **Chapter 7**).

Now the above breakdown is only meant to be a helpful guide as not everyone shares the same market. Profession, age and geographical catchment area can change the stats. It's true for example that a higher proportion of IT jobs are found through agencies. It's true that the older you get the more proactive you have to become, but then the more contacts you are likely to have, and it's also true that in some remote, insular or parochial communities around the world networking is 90% of anyone's market - it has been said that in Wales if you play rugby and sing in the choir you'll always be in work. And of course not all job hunters are of interest to search firms. But if we take these stats at face value, and there are few reasons not to, two things become obvious:

1. If all your actions comprise responding to job ads and using agencies then you're ambulance chasing and ignoring 65% of your market. You must do an element of these things of course - why would you ignore a combined 35% of your market? But don't hold your breath, as they are frighteningly competitive. The other thing they have in common is that the 'job' has been defined and also the 'person' they are seeking. They are now casting around for someone to 'shoe-horn' into that definition. That's not an economical way to job hunt and nor is it an economical way to recruit people. But that's the 'visible' jobs market for you.

Another big downside is that the recruitment process can take months, where you're being made to jump through one hoop after another, only to find yourself left hugging an empty sack because they've offered the job to one of your competitors or decided not to hire anyone at all.

2. 65% of jobs never become public knowledge and hence available to fair and open competition. This is why when you look at the paucity of job ads and see the number of agencies going bust you can get a very skewed impression of the number of jobs available at any given moment.

In a buyer's market, and it's been a buyers market for years, why should such a buyer choose to go through the costly and time consuming performance of advertising that they have a need? In a seller's market you'll see a much higher proportion of job ads and more prosperous agencies - but that's going back too far for anyone to remember. In this 'hidden market' you will by its very nature go down many blind alleyways - after all, this is no different to any other market in that not everyone, or anyone, will want to buy everything, or anything, you are selling at any given moment, and that's no reflection on you or your 'product'. That's just the way it is. But when that bit of luck kicks in and you get it right on the button it's then that the balance of power shifts in your favour because the chances are high that you won't be competing with anyone. The buyer is also more likely to make the job fit you and not the other way around - you can end up writing your own job description.

Another benefit of the 'hidden' jobs market is that the recruitment process is invariably far less protracted because you're not being made to jump through all the hoops with your competitors. It's also far, far easier to change career direction through the hidden market than it ever is through the 'visible' market. Tell a recruitment firm that you want to change career direction and watch their eyes glaze over.

It would be quite wrong to see the above four 'cylinders' of the job search engine as operating independently. They all *complement* each other and this is why we must take a broad view on what 'networking' is all about. For example, one of your troops may alert you to a job advertisement you had not seen. You can't be everywhere and if you've spent much of your time running around from one agency to another then other opportunities may have passed you by. Another on your list may be able to give you inside information about an embryonic job opportunity due to be advertised or handed over to an agency in a few weeks time. You can now take an action in the form of a direct approach to that company.

Others may recommend an agency to you that gave them good service when they were last job hunting. If any or all of the above networking actions were to result in a job offer then were they achieved through responding to an ad, making a direct approach, using an agency or through networking? You wouldn't care too much by then of course. You'd most likely think that you had just got lucky.

Allocate Your Time To Fit Your Market

One of the things we lose when we lose a job is the routine that went with it so it's critical to instil a routine of your own when you're job hunting and it must be one built around your market 'engine' as you see it. You can thrash around and kick up a lot of dust during a job search and easily delude yourself into believing you are doing something meaningful and productive when you are in reality accomplishing very little.

Displacement activity is also your enemy. For example, it's all too easy to become 'agency dependent' and spend 90% of your time chasing 20% of your market. It might make you feel good because it sure keeps you busy but it makes no sense. And it's too easy to spend all day sitting in front of your computer doing 'research', thinking you've put in a full shift, forgetting that job hunting is essentially a human activity and that you should be out there communicating.

Now this doesn't mean that you should be spending 40% of your time every week out and about talking to people as that might be raising the bar too far, but certainly you should be spending 40% of your time *thinking* about it and *planning* your actions - that's time worth investing, as we shall see in **Chapter 5**.

It's well worth planning your week ahead and dedicating a specific amount of time to firing on all four cylinders, but no more than 15% of it on scouring the job ads and responding to them. As with all campaigns you have to be flexible enough to change your plans at any given moment but don't wake up on a Monday morning and ask yourself what you're going to do that day - the chances are high that you'll end up doing anything but job hunting.

The Strength Of Weak Ties

When reviewing your troops at Stage 1 you were self-disciplined enough not to make judgments about their potential usefulness but you have to make those judgments at some point. Stage 2 is that point. You now need to marshal your troops into some kind of order, otherwise you would not know where to start. Make a second list of names of those troops on your Stage 1 list who, for one reason or another, you believe to be potentially the most informative and supportive. We will call them your 'special forces'.

It's most likely that these troops *will* be the more senior and influential, and perhaps be in your profession but you may have lost touch with them or you feel uncomfortable about approaching them. No matter, don't let negative thoughts stop you from bringing them forwards onto your Stage 2 list. Now of course you may still, in your ignorance, be leaving troops on your Stage 1 list that could, if only you knew it, be more informative than you imagine. Conversely, you may identify someone who you believe would be *too* helpful. This might be the one who you're certain would offer you a job immediately but you would prefer them not to, at least not this early in your campaign, so you might decide it would be unwise to call them up right now.

But you only know what you know and it may not matter that much because you are not eliminating these troops - *you are keeping them in reserve*. This is a critical part of your strategy because at Stage 3 you will initially deploy your 'special forces' but will find, and this is in the nature of networking, that some, perhaps many, will turn out to be not quite as helpful as you had hoped. It is then that you must call up some of your reserves and deploy them. The key to this is that you should always have a body of troops going with you throughout your campaign, but they won't always be the same people. It's now easy to see why many job hunters say 'I've done my networking'. They are the ones who skipped Stage 1 and have no reserves upon which to call.

Much useful and revealing research has been done on networking in relation to getting a job, most notably by Mark Granovetter of Stanford University, who coined the memorable term 'The Strength of Weak Ties'.

Granovetter's studies revealed that in getting a job through networking, acquaintances (weak ties) were much more influential than close friends (strong ties). In other words, the more people you know who *aren't close to you* the stronger your network is likely to be. This apparent paradox has a critical bearing on which troops you choose to put on your Stage 2 list, and has a particular resonance for those seeking to change their career.

This idea of 'connectedness' is taken up and explored in an entertaining article by Malcolm Gladwell in the 'New Yorker' (Gladwell.com). Gladwell cites Granovetter and in particular Stanley Milgram of Harvard, from whose studies originated the concept of 'six degrees of separation'. But as Gladwell states -'Six degrees of separation doesn't simply mean that everyone is linked to everyone else in six steps. It means that a very small number of people are linked to everyone else in a few steps, and the rest of us are linked to the world through those few.' It's too simplistic then to say that 'the more connections you have the better'.

It's surely no coincidence that the game 'Six Degrees of Kevin Bacon' became the exemplar for this idea of connectedness, for the acting profession is analogous here as it is always a buyer's market and notoriously 'network dependant'. As an actor you can't afford to be a 'loner' and reluctant about building your network. Good roles are few and far between and some hugely talented actors never get beyond 'walk on' or 'spear carrier' roles. When did you last see a job advertised for someone to play 'King Lear'? It's a close-knit, incestuous business where reputations can be built or broken over lunch. Actors are never 'unemployed'; they are either 'resting' or 'writing a novel'. Two out of work actors meet each other -

> 'What are you doing?'
>
> 'I'm writing a novel'
>
> 'Neither am I!'

Actors who desire to go places and 'extend their range' work hard not to become 'stereotyped' because they know that this will limit their potential for getting work in the future. So those who deliberately create diverse careers for themselves are more or less constantly in demand not simply because they become recognised and valued for 'their range' but because they *build up a breadth and depth of connectedness with a diverse range of people*, particularly 'weak ties', across the industry as a whole.

There is of course a lot more to it than that, not least 'talent' and the 'likeability factor' but just about every successful actor will attribute their success to a 'lucky break' at an early stage in their career. Why didn't the just as talented and likeable 'spear carrier' get that break? It is perhaps true that luck is where hard work meets opportunity. Your job search campaign is no different.

This is all very relevant to the rest of us who are seeking work in less exotic industries ('For all the world's a stage') because these days change is happening at such a pace that it doesn't pay to become a specialist in a small market that may have a 'short run', or even a 'long run', because when the show comes to an end and we lose our jobs we typically lack flexibility, are not seen as adaptable, have few transferable skills, have allowed other skills to atrophy, have minimal 'strong' or 'weak' ties and are isolated or marginalised. It's then time to 'not write that novel'.

The main lesson to learn from all this is that research tells us it is your *acquaintances*, rather than members of your 'inner circle', who are more likely to have access to information and other people, that can help you win your battle. Think carefully about this then when compiling your Stage 1 and 2 lists.

---------◆ ◆ ◆ ---------

CHAPTER 5

Stage 3 - Tell Them There's A War On

This is where the bullet's start flying. This is also where the reluctant networkers allow their campaign to stall. Firstly, let's be crystal clear about your objective at Stage 3. Your only objective is to find a way to let your troops know there's a war on. Once you have achieved that objective it's job done. Stage 3 need go no further than that. Now these 'ways' can sometimes be straightforward- you simply get on the phone and tell them. Other ways have to be subtle, creative and even downright devious, but for all the right reasons as explained in **Chapter 1**. Your tactics in letting your troops know there's a war on must not be a matter of 'one size fits all'. How you network one person may be markedly different from how you network another. It will all depend on the nature of the relationship you have with the person and how you feel about it. You may need to proceed with caution.

It is reassuring to the reluctant networker that it isn't always necessary at Stage 3 to ask your troops to, for example, 'keep your eyes and ears open' or do anything for you at all for that matter. The reality is this, and experience bears this out all the time - either this person is going to be helpful or he/she is not. That's about the size of it. Yes, some may need a little coaxing but those willing to 'step up to the plate' will do so, without you having to ask them to do anything, and the ones who are not will not - and no amount of pleading from you will change their mind. And it's right here that you find out who your friends (or acquaintances) really are. It's right now that you are either disappointed or totally surprised by their reaction. Stage 3 then takes a certain amount of courage on your part; you've got let your troops know there's a war on and let the cards fall where they may. But it also takes the pain out of it.

Stopping The Lights From Going Out

It's pretty obvious that if your contacts are unaware that you are in the jobs market then they are not going to come to you with any information that might help your cause. At this stage you are likely to have three categories of contacts:

- Those contacts, probably your *close friends*, who know there's a war on because you have already told them (whether you have gone about it in the right way we'll put to one side for now)

- Those who don't know and you're confident there's no way they could have heard about it from anyone else. Your next-door neighbour will often fit into that category.
- Those contacts, perhaps your *acquaintances*, who you're pretty sure will have heard about it but not from you. In effect they will have heard it through the grapevine or network.

Now it's that last category that's worth paying some attention to because you can't be certain what they have been told and, alarmingly, *misinformation* about you and your situation can get passed around your network, by well meaning people, and the lights could be going out all over the place without you even knowing it. Let's explore just some of the conversations that typically happen without your knowledge:

ENVY

Troop 1: Have you heard that Bill's lost his job?

Troop 2: Never! What's he going to do?

Troop 1: Oh, he'll be ok. He'll be laughing all the way to the bank.

Troop 2: Yeah, I guess. He's been there a few years. Lucky dog!

Yes, there are people who will be envious of you. They do the sums and assume you'll be living high on the hog, and that of course may be far from the truth.

MISUNDERSTANDING

Troop 3: Bill's lost his job!

Troop 4: Wow - that's great timing for him.

Troop 3: How do you mean?

Troop 4: Well, he's coming up for retirement anyway.

Troop 3: You're kidding - how old is he?

Troop 4: Not sure about that, but he's been around forever.

If it weren't bad enough losing your job at 55 it rubs salt in the wound if all your contacts assume you'll be sipping Pina-Colada beachside in Acapulco, when in reality you'd stack shelves in Wal-Mart or fight someone for the chance of operating the paint-mixing machine in your local DIY store.

RESPECT

Troop 5: Have you heard Bill's lost his job?

Troop 6: No! What do you think he'll do?

Troop 5: Bill? He'll get snapped up. He really knows his stuff.

Troop 6: Your right - he's pretty damn good is Bill.

Well, it sure is nice to know that you're held in such high regard.

THEIR COMPLACENCY

Troop 7: Bill's looking for a job.

Troop 8: Yes, I heard but he'll be ok - he knows everyone.

Troop 7: Yeah, he's well connected.

Now you're not in on that conversation to say 'I do know a lot of people and you're two of them so don't think you can't come to me with information'. Ironic.

YOUR COMPLACENCY

Troop 9: Has Bill found a job yet?

Troop 10: No - he hasn't started looking yet. He's taking a few months off re-charging the old batteries.

Troop 9: Oh - I thought he'd started looking.

You may have told Troop 9 some time ago that there was a war on but you may have told troop 10 that you *might* take some time out for a break. Don't confuse your troops as it stops the flow of information. There may be some people with whom you would prefer to be a bit more bullish and suggest that there's no reason to panic. It's a pride thing. But information is power and it can work for you or against you. What information you choose to release to your troops must be measured and consistent, not least because they may be communicating with each other. You may well choose to take some time out before starting your campaign but there's always the danger that you can soon become history. There's also an important distinction to be made here. Although these contacts of yours may have heard that you've left your previous employment, *that's not the same as them knowing that there's a war on.*

CHINESE WHISPERS

Troop 11: Bill's lost his job!

Troop 12: What - again? That's tough.

Troop 11: No, he's ok. He's fixed up.

Troop 12: No! Who with?

Troop 11: He's operating the paint-mixing machine down at the DIY store.

Troop 12: Well, he sure lands on his feet that guy.

Now, you may well have told Troop 11 a few weeks ago that you were off to a final interview. She may have wished you good luck. You were unsuccessful but you haven't got back to her. She assumed you were successful and now gives others the good news. Don't pester people with your job search but don't leave them swinging in the breeze either.

FEAR

Troop 13: Bill's lost his job!

Troop 14: Never!

Troop 13: Yep - a bit messy by all accounts.

Troop 14: Wow! Do you think I should call him?

Troop 13: No. I was going to but what do you say? It's probably the last thing he wants.

So, some of your contacts may have heard exaggerated accounts, or accurate accounts for that matter, about the circumstances of your exit and you may feel real fine about the whole thing but they would rather not make that call if they feel that by so doing they might light the blue touch paper.

If you feel deeply disappointed that troops 1-14 above haven't contacted you, when you had every reason to expect them to, well, now you know why. And if you are a person of a certain age who has taken 'early retirement' from your previous employment then take care because if you are campaigning it's unwise to use the phrase 'early retirement' in any context, as it can sow the seeds of confusion in the minds of others. You don't want your troops to think you're not serious about it and you sure don't want potential buyers of your talents to believe that you might not give 100% commitment to the task or think they can get you on the cheap. Loose talk costs jobs so you're either in the jobs market or you are not.

Lining Up Your Referees

When your campaign reaches a successful conclusion and you win the prize of a job offer then you are most likely to be asked to provide written or verbal references. Now it can be a big mistake to leave this to the end of the campaign as opportunities can be missed. Stories are legion of job seekers having a tough campaign going on for months, finally achieving an offer, being asked for references, approaching a referee asking if they would be good enough to give a reference, only to be met with the response 'Of course I'll give you a reference - how long have you been job hunting? A year! Why didn't you approach me a year ago - I could have used you in my business?' Why didn't you approach them a year ago? Maybe because it's something you thought had to be done at the end of the campaign, or most likely you didn't think about it at all.

Given that your referees are likely to be people of influence this is a most benign, even flattering way of

meeting, and your instincts and judgment will inform you on this, but with certain contacts it might be best if you wait to see if *they* suggest it. Most certainly, if there's a possibility that you could find yourself working in *their* organisation then *they will need time* to consider the implications of that, of which there are many. A bull in a china shop approach; ('...any vacancies in your company?') can be wholly counter-productive.

It's quite common, after letting one of your troops know there's a war on, to get a call from them a few hours or even days later suggesting a meeting. They may, for example, have needed time to confer with another person about the way forward and many of your contacts would not want to give you false hope and raise your expectations about what they might be able to do for you. You can always be reassured that there is after all a Stage 4 still to come. This 'slow burn' element is of primary importance when deciding your actions throughout your campaign. Choosing the right medium through which to communicate with your troops is therefore critical.

The 'Thank You And Goodbye' E-mail

This is a good example of when the e-mail might be a better way of letting certain troops know that there's a war on. It's extremely important that when you leave a job you inform others of your intentions.

You may have built up good relationships with acquaintances both inside and outside your organisation. They may be business partners, stakeholders, customers, clients, and suppliers. They may even be people you have never met and yes, it can be very easy to network people you have never met, as it's not difficult to build those good working relationships by telephone and e-mail. Such people can feel most offended if you were to leave without telling them, personally, that you are moving on. They wouldn't want to hear it from a third party a few weeks down the line.

Closing it all down well is then both a courtesy and a professional necessity - your reputation is at stake here. Also you do want to avoid misinformation, assumptions and bad news flying around without you realising it.

Don't take the lazy route here by copying the same e-mail to everyone as it lacks that personal touch. Be prepared to invest your time into each one. Now of course what you say in those e-mails will depend entirely on the relationship you have with that person. But the kind of message that goes down well is '.... You will have heard by now I'm sure that there's been a few changes around here but now that the dust has settled I want to let you know personally that I'll be leaving at the end of March and I'm now starting a serious job search! It's been great working with you and I hope you've found it as fruitful as I have. Who knows what the future holds, we may do so again some time...'

'I'm now starting a serious job search!' does inject a little humour into the message and yet it is the most important part - your contact can now be under no illusion that there's a war on, so job done. This e-mail can be sent retrospectively and with some contacts you can say this: ' I did my best to leave everything squared off at my end before leaving but time was limited and I don't want to leave anyone swinging in the breeze, so if you need any information or advice don't hesitate to e-mail or call me on...'. Rather perversely you are asking if you can do anything for them, not the other way around, despite your having all the stress and anxiety a job search can bring. These 'thank you and goodbye e-mails' do elicit a lot of positive responses and can open up opportunities further down the track that you wouldn't believe. Also remember that these troops may be 'weak ties'.

Learning From The Experience Of Others

Given that there's a limit to how many of your troops you can ask to be a referee for you we have to be a lot more creative. Some, or indeed many, of your troops may be quite 'battle hardened' themselves so it's well worth going through the names and asking yourself 'how many of my troops have, to my knowledge, had a battle of their own to fight over the last few years?' One of the most frustrating things about the job search is its notoriety for lack of meaningful feedback. Because of this we don't always learn from our own mistakes. It's far better, surely, to learn from the mistakes made by others? Now, with this approach you can open up the flow of information quite painlessly as it's a benign way of letting your troops know there's a war on. You can call or e-mail certain contacts and ask them for information/advice/feedback on just about any aspect of *their* previous campaigns that you care to think about. For example;

- **When you were job hunting did you come across any good agencies/search firms?** If your contacts are able to provide you with the name of someone in an agency who gave them good service when they were job hunting then that's a real bonus. The most important thing though is that you've opened up a line of communication with your contact who can now be in no doubt that there's a war on. The conversation may then move in a direction you could never have predicted. But, as we'll see at Stage 4, it doesn't matter at all what direction the conversation takes.

- **I'm actively job hunting and I'm going to make a direct approach to XYZ Company - didn't you work for them a while back and do you know who it would be best for me to write to?** If your contact can give you sound advice about whom to pitch your direct approach then that's a bonus. But don't be disappointed if they say 'No, I've lost touch with them' - allow the conversation to go wherever it goes because they now know there's a war on. Allow for the 'slow burn' because they may call you back and say ' I've spoken to one of my contacts and got a name for you.' When you really get this on the hot button your contact may say ' Yes, I know him well - don't write to him, send me your CV/résumé and I'll stick it under his nose. He'll meet you.' Well, with any luck that's another job they won't have to advertise.

- **I'm off to a job interview next week and I'm feeling real rusty. You went to interviews a while back - what kind of questions were they asking?** When your campaign gets up a head of steam Stage 3 networking gets easier. Opportunities arise to contact certain troops who may have previously proved tricky to contact. Unsurprisingly, many people have horror stories to recount, and they love to tell them, about interviews they attended during their campaigns, and from which much can be learnt. And of course your troops can tell you what worked *well* for them in their campaigns - tactics and strategies that you might want to replicate.

- **I'm job hunting and trying to get to grips with this technology stuff. These online job sites weren't around the last time I was in the market - did you find them useful and are there any you can recommend?** Through protracted trial and error you can find your way through the morass of online services available but we know that campaigning is time critical so short circuit all that by asking others what they found effective or otherwise.

- **Have you interviewed people for jobs? What questions do you ask and what are you looking for?** Don't ignore the good advice that may be available to you from those contacts of yours who may have experience of recruitment, interviewing, advertising for jobs and using agencies from the client company perspective. Their information and advice can give you real and valuable insight.

There are alternative ways of discovering information. Of course there are. It could be strongly argued that there is almost too much information available to us, perhaps at the click of a mouse or the faintest touch of a screen. But that is to forget that this isn't a battle best fought at a distance. Networking success requires close engagement. It requires interaction with real human beings. You need to see the whites of their eyes. This is not to deny the huge benefits technology can bring to your campaign but tell all those people who want to be your friends on social and other networking sites that you need a job and then sit back and discover who your friends really are. The silence can be deafening. And as we have discovered, it is those *acquaintances* on LinkedIn that are likely to be more fruitful.

Tracking People Down

There will no doubt be troops on your Stage 1 and Stage 2 list with whom you have lost touch, but who could be good allies if only they knew there was a war on. Tracking them down can be time consuming and be a real test of your sleuth like abilities.

A great deal of your time networking may be devoted to this and yes, you must utilise Google, Facebook, LinkedIn etc in your campaign, but yet again you may miss opportunities through over-reliance on technology. You can 'kill two birds with one stone' by approaching someone on your list who may know the whereabouts of someone with whom you have lost contact, and these conversations are so painless:

You: This is a bit of a long shot but I need to speak with Jim and we've lost touch. Do you have his number?

Answer: No, I haven't met Jim for a couple of years. How are you doing?

You: Ok thanks, but I'm in the jobs market. That's why I need to contact Jim.

Answer: Oh! I'm surprised - I'd heard you'd left but I overheard someone saying you were working at the DIY store - operating the paint-mixing machine?

You: No - I just mentioned it as a possibility. Didn't get it.

Answer - Hard luck - let's have lunch.

This can be a good way of activating those troops who you thought would have contacted you but didn't because they were switched off by another. On the other hand your contact may well have had Jim's number and that would have been useful information for you to have. At worst you have opened up a line of communication, told someone there's a war on and thus opened up the possibility of information flowing your way either immediately or at a later stage after the 'slow burn'. You've also maybe got lunch.

You may be very loosely connected to people in high places, the real movers and shakers, but that connection might be so loose that even if you had their number or e-mail address you wouldn't, as a reluctant networker, feel right about contacting them. Well, just maybe there's another on your list much better placed to tell them there's a war on:

You: Do you ever bump into ol' Barack?

Answer: Yeah, every couple of months.

You: Well, next time you meet him you might drop into the conversation that I'm in the market?

Answer: Sure, leave it to me - I'll fix it.

You: Be discrete - don't mention the paint-mixing debacle.

Keep A Smile On Your Face And A Spring In Your Step

You must always remember that this is your battle, you are the General and it's critical that you are seen to be leading from the front. However tough things are getting you must always keep a smile on your face and a spring in your step. Enthusiasm really is infectious - if you've got it they will catch it. But so is depression. There's no advantage to be gained by communicating to your troops that 'it's really tough out there' or give reasons why something can't be done. If your general behaviour is exemplary and you remain upbeat then they will stay with you. Any signals from you that this battle is going to end in failure then your troops will thin out because *no one wants to hear bad news and bad news travels fast.*

Don't bore them to death with your campaign either. If you raise the subject every time you meet then the next time they see you coming they'll run for cover. It happens the other way around too. One of the 'downsides' of good networking is that you constantly have people asking 'Have you got a job yet?' You really won't want to hear that every day but it is a positive sign. The time to worry is when your troops stop asking the question.

Release information to your troops selectively and don't tell anyone anything they don't need to know. This is simply to ensure that misinformation isn't passed around your network that might confuse others or switch them off entirely. This is particularly important if you are campaigning within either a close-knit community or a limited market where people know each other.

Even the way you dress can have a positive or negative impact on others. If you look good you'll feel good and if you feel good you'll perform well. When you are out and about in business hours, networking face to face with people on their territory, you must always be prepared for that chance encounter - that unexpected but welcome introduction/referral to one of your troop's contacts. They would be unlikely, even embarrassed, to make that introduction if you didn't look the part. You don't get a second chance to make a first impression and first impressions are visual.

And finally, do remember not to switch your troops off after to going to all the trouble to switch them on. When those envious people subsequently say 'I bet it's real nice to have all that spare time' don't respond in the affirmative by telling them that you are doing all those jobs around the house that have been stacking up over the years. Respond by saying 'I wish - I now know why they call job hunting a full time job in itself - there's not enough hours in the day.' That's not a signal of desperation; it's a signal to them that you are leading from the front. There's no room for ambivalence.

--------- ◆ ◆ ◆ ---------

CHAPTER 6

Stage 4 - Give Them The Ammunition

All the actions you took at Stage 3 can now be followed up at this the 4th and final stage. Your organisational, administrative and general record keeping skills come to the fore when networking. You simply must keep accurate records of all actions taken, calls made, e-mails sent and meetings held. Dates, times, locations, a record of what took place and follow up actions to be taken and by whom must be recorded, otherwise you will get into a right mess and confusion will reign.

There is little point in telling your troops there's a war on if you don't follow it up by sending them some ammunition, which in this context is your CV/résumé. This may not always be appropriate and allow yourself to be guided by your own judgment on this. It can be quite a revelation how little some people know about who we are and what we actually do. We often define ourselves, and allow others to define us, by our job titles, many of which are meaningful in one organisation but meaningless in another. Have you ever noticed how, when you ask people what they do, they never tell you - they tell you what they *are*? Now, this is a kind of convenient social shorthand, which suits both parties. After all, if a teacher actually told you what they *did* it would take all day. But when you're in the jobs market your troops need as much clarity as you dare to give.

Many of your troops will end a Stage 3 conversation by saying they will 'keep their eyes and ears open' which is fine, but you should then think about just how much they know about you and what they should be looking for.

Accept All Information Gracefully

Through lack of clarity and understanding well meaning troops will enthusiastically give you information that is off the mark. For example they may show you a copy of a job ad that holds no interest for you. It's essential that you handle this with sensitivity. Never, ever, reject out of hand any information, advice or recommendations that come your way. Should you do so then it's most likely that you may never hear from that contact again. They will retire hurt from the fray and will not subsequently come up with that one gem of information that could have proved to be a defining moment in your campaign.

Accept everything gratefully, always let your contacts know that you have actioned their information in some way, and maybe at a later stage tactfully re-educate them about your intentions. If you are a reluctant networker then the chances are high that you are not big on self promotion, not that status conscious perhaps, not much given to telling others where you sit on any social scale or hierarchy. Well, modesty is a wonderful trait to have in life generally but it won't serve you well in the jobs market, not least because many of your troops may have little idea of what you are capable of. What better way for the reluctant networker to get this message across than by sending a copy of the CV / résumé?

The Follow Up Email

Now, tactically, you might want to leave, say, a two-week gap between Stage 3 and Stage 4 because that buys you the time to see which of these troops are going to be more proactive than others. Some of your troops may respond immediately at Stage 3 by requesting your résumé/CV in which case you send it immediately. Although two weeks may seem a long time to you it's a short time for everyone else so don't panic if you don't hear anything back for a while.

There is such a thing as the 'phoney war', which is the time period between telling your troops there's a war on and any information actually flowing back to you. This can be disconcerting but it is quite natural, not least because your troops have their own lives to lead and your job search is never top of their agenda. But if you wanted to generate a bit more activity now might be the time to e-mail your CV/résumé to your contact.

Now of course what you say in that e-mail will depend entirely on who these contacts are, and your relationship with them. But it might go something like this:

'...Thanks for your time on the phone the other week and thanks very much for saying that you'd keep your eyes and ears open. It's subsequently occurred to me that you might not be that up to speed about my huge range of talents so I'm attaching my résumé - difficult for me to be objective about it but I think I've got it right, though any

feedback you might want to give on it would be
appreciated. If you spot any typo's let me know!
Incidentally, if you happen to come across anyone who you
think might have an interest in someone with my
background do feel free to pass the résumé on to them.'

Much of your networking correspondence can be quite light hearted in this way but nevertheless serious signals are being sent. Asking for feedback can be most valuable as your contact may be able to identify things that you have done that you had completely forgotten and omitted from your résumé. If you have made a typing error then you'd be the last person to spot it. In suggesting these things you are encouraging them to read your sales literature and by so doing get a clearer picture of your talents, skills, level etc.

That final paragraph is critical because there's little point in sending this ammunition to your troops if you don't give them the 'green light' to pass it on to *their* troops. Many of your troops might see your résumé as being for 'their eyes only' and might be reluctant to pass it on to others without your express permission, and they haven't always got the time to call you up to check. Because of this many opportunities can be missed. Note how carefully that final paragraph is worded. It would be far too crude to write '...Incidentally, I'd be grateful if you could pass my résumé on to your contacts.' That would be putting pressure on them and giving them work to do. The caveats soften the message: *'Incidentally, if you happen* ('don't make this your mission as I appreciate you are busy but if luck should have it') *to come across anyone* (don't even use the word 'contacts') *who you think might* (they might not but it doesn't matter) *have an interest* (never use the words 'job', 'vacancy', 'role', 'opening') *in someone* (not necessarily me) *with my background* (deliberately not job specific - interpret my background as you wish) *do feel free to pass the résumé on to them* (You are also free not to do so).

Have The Self-Discipline To Lose Control

In just about any other sphere of activity during the **Action** half of your campaign it is important that you retain as much control as you can. With Stage 4 networking however feel free to *lose* control. It has been said for example that if you give your troops carte blanche to fire off your résumé to their troops then you lose control over where it is going, which of

81

course you do but there is no downside to this. The worst that can happen is that it lands on someone's desk who isn't interested. Well, that happens much of the time anyway.

One of the signs of good networking is getting a call from a complete stranger asking if you would care to meet with them to discuss a need they have that they believe you could fulfil '...I've read your résumé...'(Who is this guy and how has he got my résumé?) Why do you care? Go along and find out from this new acquaintance of yours. Incidentally, that changes the 'dynamic' between the seller and buyer as the 'balance of power' has shifted in favour of the seller. As the seller you don't now have to do such an overt selling job on the buyer as you would have done if responding to an advertisement. This is when 'buyers' may have to become 'sellers' in order to encourage you to take the job.

Successful job hunting doesn't come cheap but it's often businesslike and courteous to hold a leaving party to which you invite as many of your troops as you can muster. Get a business card printed with your name and contact numbers on it - these are neat and efficient little devices to hand out at such events.

Work that room. What better than to get your contacts all in one place at the same time?

See all this as an investment in your campaign and not a cost. You may be leaving your present organisation as a result of a major restructuring in which case attend as many leaving parties as you can. Work other people's rooms. They are all potential converts to your cause. This is not the time to hide away in the shadows or on the margins. Isolation is a killer. Every one of those people could have information and advice that would make a welcome addition to your bank of knowledge and help raise your game.

Be receptive and ensure that you don't come across to others as being set in your ways and closed to ideas, for those ideas will stop flowing - you can do this through body language alone - a dismissive look from you can be like turning off a tap. If a number of you are in the jobs market it can be extremely effective if you agree to have a regular fortnightly meeting to share market intelligence, research, swap stories, give feedback on each other's résumés, gather information etc. What wasted opportunities there might be if you were all out in the market fighting your own battles independently, gathering information, and learning nothing from each other? There is strength in solidarity. This can get problematic if you were competing with each other in the same market but nothing that can't be overcome if common sense is applied.

Travel First Class - It Gets Results

If you are job-hunting from home make it a rule to get out and about and physically put yourself in potentially rewarding situations. Chance encounters with strangers can of course have risks - going for a stroll through the local park at 3am is not to be recommended. But be prepared to seize opportunities. For example, if you are on your way to an interview and get talking to a fellow traveller then make a point of telling this new troop of yours (that all important 'weak tie') that you are going to an interview. You've gone straight to Stage 3! If you hit it off then give them that shiny new business card - that meeting could turn out to be an informal interview in itself.

Every journey you take is then a recruitment drive and an opportunity to enlist the help of strangers. I know of one enterprising job hunter, who never travelled first class, yet who *invested* in a 3 month first class train season ticket and took the journey into town every morning and back again in the evening, engaging fellow first class commuters in meaningful conversation. He had a job offer within a month and got a refund on his ticket. Bravo. What chutzpah. Take a bow. He also *invested* in some smart new clothes, spending twice the amount of money than he would normally have done. Well, you've got to look the part and why not travel first class - as we know they haven't got where they are by being backwards in coming forwards.

If you dress as if you're on your uppers and always travel steerage then don't be surprised if you find yourself at the bottom. Successful self marketing has much to do with perception - if it looks like a duck, walks like a duck and makes a noise like a duck then it's a duck. Raise your game.

---------◆ ◆ ◆ ---------

CHAPTER 7
Using The Information

There is no 'Stage 5' as such because once you have taken your troops through to Stage 4 you then have to manage the process as best you can. We saw in Chapter 3 that some of your troops will not be as forthcoming with information as you had hoped and it is post Stage 4 that you will be bringing forwards some reserves from your Stage 1 list and taking them through Stage 3 and then Stage 4. This Chapter will give you some ideas about how to handle the information that might flow your way.

Handling Referrals

Some of the 'hot' information that comes your way will be in the form of a referral i.e. your contacts suggest that you get in touch with their contacts. To get this right it may well be worth asking your contacts for their advice on the best way to go about this, not least because they themselves may not have given it much thought and you certainly don't want to get it wrong.

Do remember that these can be sensitive situations and the credibility and reputation of your contact is always on the line, as is your credibility and reputation. Choosing the right medium to communicate is just as important in these situations as it is at Stage 3. Don't be too quick to pick that phone up and call them, as e-mail might be better. If you do call them up then think about the timing. As a rule it's best perhaps not to call people up during working hours, as they are likely to be busy. What are their working hours? You might want to send a preliminary e-mail to set up a mutually convenient time for that call. You may suggest to your contact that the three of you get together socially for an informal introductory meeting.

Before doing anything at all you might be wise to do some background research on that person and their business. You may even have other troops who might know this person. Does the person you are going to meet have the power to hire you or are they a gatekeeper who might have to refer you on to someone else?

These are all things that the introverted networker would be wise to consider that might not occur to the more extroverted networker who may have a more 'flash bang wallop' approach to networking, and who invariably ends up wondering why they are left standing out in the cold.

If you do make that call have clarity on your objective, which would almost certainly be to get them to agree to meet you, so at the earliest opportunity make that suggestion and then get off the phone. Your objective is not to get bogged down being 'interviewed' over the phone, nor to sound off about your 'above the line' objectives (Chapter 2). Get a meeting with them, at which you will drill down on what they see as their problem and then demonstrate why you might be the one to help them solve it.

How you handle the meeting itself is not within the remit of this book but is fully explained in 'Winning At Interview'.

After the meeting with a new contact you will, after making your notes, consider sending a 'thank you' e-mail, confirming your interest in having further discussions, dealing with any issues raised or not raised at the meeting and reminding them of any commitment made to you about what happens next and when. You may copy this to your original contact or independently let that contact know how the meeting went. Again, don't pester your troops but nor must you leave them 'out of the loop' after they have gone to the trouble of helping you.

Handling Leads

Information will most often come to you in the form of a 'lead' rather than a referral. Such leads may be 'hot', 'warm' or 'cold'.

Hot Lead: One of your contacts may have information that a specific vacancy has arisen at their place of work and they can give you accurate information about that vacancy and tell you exactly who the right person is for you to call or write to. Your contact may even be able to make a personal introduction. If their advice is for you to write to the hiring manager then ask if you can use *their* name at the beginning of your letter.

Never use people's names without their express permission. Unless you can think of a good reason not to, then always write a letter as speed is not usually critical in these situations and a letter on good quality paper is more classy and professional. A letter also has a certain novelty value. Some people take the view that writing a letter these days is quaint if not eccentric, and you may be one of them, in which case don't do it. Be guided by your instincts on this but do remember that successful job hunting isn't about doing what everyone else does, and see *'Turning Cold Leads Into Hot Opportunities'* below.

Warm Lead: One of your contacts may have information from a third party (unknown to you) about an actual or possible vacancy at the third party's place of work or maybe (getting less warm now) at a fourth party's place of work. It's normally best to resist writing to the target organisation until you have followed the networking trail and hopefully got a meeting, or at least had a telephone conversation, with that third or fourth party. Hiring managers are more likely to meet with you if you have come 'referred' through even a quite long list of contacts.

The information you get from both 'hot' and 'warm' leads is rarely in the public domain.

Cold Lead: This can encompass a very broad range of information that arrives from your troops. It is typically information in the public domain but not spotted by you. However active a job hunter you can't be everywhere all the time and the reality is that powerful information will pass you by every day. It is these cold leads that might impel you to make an independent direct approach to the hiring organization. We saw in Chapter 4 that making these approaches is by no means the 'last throw of the dice', although 'job beggars' believe otherwise. Oh no, they are right up there with, and closely aligned to, networking itself. Because of this, we will take a closer look at how to make such approaches.

Turning Cold Leads Into Hot Opportunities

Let's assume that you're starting with a blank sheet and really want to set your mind to making direct approaches. You've set the hares running with your networking but you quite rightly want to do your bit and not spend much time ambulance chasing. You want to be *proactive* not reactive. You know that job ad you found the other day didn't crop up overnight, and how come that head-hunter knew about that job vacancy and you didn't?

Imagine you had a crystal ball and knew what job ads were going to turn up over the next three months, that you knew for sure what these recruitment firms were going to get their sticky hands on - why, you'd sure have the inside track then and be able to head them all off at the pass. You'd be delirious with pure unalloyed joy. Well, in the absence of that crystal ball you'll just have to bring some imagination and creativity to your campaign.

What's your objective here? What is it you want to achieve with a direct approach? Well, in its purist form you want to identify a need within your target hiring organization in the time frame between when *they've* identified it but *before* they get around to doing anything about it. That's about it. But also, and as we'll see later, given that some people don't know they need something until you start selling it to them, you may be smart enough to identify the need before *they* know they've got it. And, just in case you've slipped out of the zone, and it's been a while since Chapter 2, their need is their problem and you are the solution.

So, how do needs arise within organizations? For what reasons and under what circumstances are jobs created or become vacant? For it's information about these reasons and circumstances that you and your troops should be seeking. Here's just a selection:

1. Expansion, diversification, relocation, restructuring, development of new products or services, government legislation, mergers, takeovers, new competitors entering the market, companies exiting a market.

2. Illness, death, maternity leave, promotion, demotion, retirement, resignations, personal career development, firings, hiring's, poor performers.

These are not exhaustive by any means and it's worth separating them into two distinct groups because information about **1** above is often in the public domain, therefore both you and your troops can read or hear about it, whereas information about **2** above is not always in the public domain and therefore more likely to come from your troops. These are the 'one-off' warm leads and are not necessarily symptomatic of any big change going on in an organization or market. And it's *change* that's the key word here.

One of the big paradoxes of the jobs market is that the changes that traditionally lose jobs for some are exactly the same as those that create jobs for others. Yes, one person's bad news can be another's brand new career. Someone once memorably said that when a man marries his mistress it automatically creates a vacancy. The jobs market is immensely complex and not an easy thing to pin down, although it's very easy to pronounce on and make it sound as if we know what we are talking about. When people ask 'What's the jobs market like?' it's easy to say 'real bad', 'pretty good' or make any other comment, all of which can be meaningless. The only accurate answer is to say 'It depends whose market we're talking about here'.

Your market may be 'real bad' but with a positive mental attitude and the guts to network you'll be ok. With low self-esteem, poor interpersonal skills and a negative mental attitude you'll struggle even in a buoyant market, but in a 'real bad' market?

Here's another paradox. A job advertisement can be one of the best sources of information from which to get a cold lead. Clues and leads can pass you by every day if you're not 'in the zone', simply because you're 'looking for a job' with a quite specific title in a quite specific area and which carries with it a quite specific pay check. So 99.99% of the time you'll say, and quite rightly, 'I don't want that job' and, quite wrongly, carry on scanning.

Learn to look at job ads more creatively than that. If you're looking for a really big problem to solve don't ignore those ads seeking junior people. Similarly, if you are that junior person looking for a small problem to solve, don't be psyched out by those ads carrying 'heavyweight' job titles. Ask yourself the really important questions such as:

- What is this organization?
- What is their business?
- Are they in my travel to work area?
- Did I know they were there?
- What is their need today?
- Why do they need it?
- How transferable are my skills?
- What could I bring to their party?
- Might they need me tomorrow?

If you've been commuting back and for to work and making the same journey for some years it's possible that you're not too familiar with what hiring organizations might be located elsewhere in your catchment area. It's well worth heading off in other directions and doing the occasional reconnaissance. You could do this through the Internet but why not get out and get some fresh air. You never know whom you might meet. Researching your travel to work area is a top priority in your campaign. Compile a list of those organizations, large, medium or small, that could conceivably use someone with your talents if not now then at some time in the future. Keep an open mind about sectors because skills, knowledge and experience are often transferable. For the older job hunter who has worked for large organizations the small to medium sized organizations can be a rewarding furrow to plough. Today's small company that wants to go places needs experienced people to take them there. Commitment is also highly prized by such organizations and that's a quality often found in the more mature person.

It's well worth keeping a dossier of information on these organizations as their names will most likely crop up in your conversations with your troops and they add more fuel to your job search engine. If one of your troops mentions a company that you should have known about but didn't then that sends the signal to them that you're not being diligent in your research and knowledge of the market, which you're not.

A job advertisement is only a snapshot in time so look at the 'preamble' because that often tells you why they have the need. And if a company is going to spend big bucks on a job ad they may as well do a big PR job on themselves while they're at it... 'As the foremost company in our field we are at the leading edge of this, that and the other and our dynamic team is now rapidly expanding...' Look at their website for more information, check out the biogs of senior staff. Your target executive, and maybe your next boss, will be among them. Why - you may even spot some old acquaintances.

If you are diligent and do all these things then good things will come to you. This is where the luck and coincidence really seems to kick in because that job search engine is topped up with fuel and you are firing on all four cylinders. That's not to say that any of this is easy. If it were easy all these career coaches and authors of books on job hunting would have to find another way of earning a buck. But like I said earlier, one person's career change is another's career opportunity. Whatever you read and whatever you hear get into the habit of asking yourself the key questions i.e. 'what are the implications of this information for my campaign?' and 'what changes would need to be taking place for this organization to need someone with my expertise?

Your objective here is to find some information, perhaps tenuous, on which to hang your hat when making your direct approach. Put yourself in the buyers' position. How impressed would you be if you received a direct approach which simply said 'I am writing to enquire if you have any vacancies in your company' and then went on to tell you what *they* were 'looking for' and which contained the same tired old clichés such as 'I am now seeking a new challenge'? Not much impressed, for that's a job-begging letter typical of those received by buyers every day and which are most often instantly consigned to the garbage can. They are letters from job hunters who have taken ownership of the problem and who are not 'in the zone'. They are unlikely to elicit a reply let alone a rejection.

A good direct approach doesn't give the reader the impression that it's just one of many sent out by the seller that day. No, It's one that clearly sends the signal that the sellers have done their homework, and have had the initiative and taken the time to do some research.

Now all of this is time consuming but you must be prepared to invest time and emotional energy into your campaign. You might take the view 'either they have a job for me or they don't so why waste my time doing all this research? I'll just fire off the same letter to all of them and see if something sticks.' That 'shotgun' approach is one taken by too many job hunters who end up with long, stressful and morale-sapping campaigns. With the 'snipers' approach one well-aimed shot is more likely to get a result so it's *quality* not quantity that really counts. You'd be better off making six well-considered quality direct approaches than six-dozen of the shotgun variety. Here are a few sample opening paragraphs to give you an idea of what you should be aiming for:

- 'Having noticed from your website that you distribute your products to businesses in the automotive, freight and shipping industries, and that you are planning to expand into the rail sector, it occurs to me that you may well have a need for someone with my skills and experience.'

- 'Your advertisement on the 21 April for a new Programme Manager indicated that you are building a dedicated team to manage the government contract won by your company in March. You may of course have the additional expertise 'in house' but having worked on similar projects my experience may be of interest to you.'

- ' A colleague recently told me that you are taking on the business that XYZ Company are outsourcing. You may therefore be looking to build on your existing team, if not now then in the near future.'

- 'You will be aware that the new Government health and safety legislation being introduced in September will have a huge impact on our sector in particular and the pressure on businesses to comply is intense. You may of course already be well up to speed on this but if not then my background may be of interest to you.'

That last example demonstrates how you can *create* a job for yourself because some people don't know they need something until you start selling it to them, or perhaps they *have* realised the need but are dragging their heels on the issue. Such approaches can galvanize them into action.

These opening paragraphs are much more businesslike and focus on the perceived needs of the buyer (and remember that these leads could have come from your 'weak ties'). They are couched in a language that is in no way intemperate or 'pushy' - no 'hard sell' that should sit well with you the reluctant networker and not least with the reader.

Note that the words 'job', 'vacancy', 'opening' 'opportunity' 'role' nor 'position' have no place in a good direct approach because they are not 'customer focussed' and your need is of no interest to the reader. A good opening paragraph should arouse the interest of the reader and you achieve this by letting them know from the outset that you have done your homework and found out something about their business, products, services, plans, issues or customers and that you can identify a link between these things and your knowledge, skills, expertise and experience.

This is not a 'technique' but a courtesy you must extend to the buyers. Note also that the opening paragraph invites the reader to read the next paragraph to find out more about your expertise. It is in this next paragraph where you 'sell the benefits' and give them perhaps a 'menu' of bullet points from which they can choose.

This paragraph can begin with the preamble 'You will see from my résumé/CV that my experience includes...' and then set out the 'menu' where you emphasise what you can bring to their party to solve the perceived problem. Because no one wants to buy everything you are selling at any given moment it's unlikely that every item on your menu will make them sit up but hopefully something will strike a chord.

One of the real arts of making a good direct approach is to *always leave the onus on the reader to decide what they might invite you in to discuss*. This strikes at the heart of one of the biggest barriers that sellers who are not 'in the zone' put in their own way and that lead to inertia ' I can't make direct approaches or even start my campaign until I've decided what job I want'. This is nonsense because a job title is just a label that a buyer chooses to give you at a given point in time. As a seller in the zone you don't have to have decided what that label is going to be. The buyer decides that. All you have to do is clarify what the skills, knowledge, talents and expertise are in your kit bag and go into battle. If you are too specific about what you want e.g. 'I am now seeking a position as...' then why would they waste your time inviting you in to discuss something better?

For this reason you might want to express in your closing paragraph that you have an 'open mind' for if you have an open mind then *they* are more likely to have an open mind. For example: ' *At this stage I have an open mind regarding type of role, tenure etc but strongly feel I can make a real contribution to your plans for expansion. For this reason I would be pleased to discuss the possibilities at perhaps an informal meeting. I can be contacted on...'*

The word 'tenure' implies that you have an open mind about the conditions under which they might want to hire you. You may be looking for what you might call a 'permanent job' but that is self-delusional for there is no such thing and hasn't been for some years. Give it whatever title you like e.g. 'permanent', 'temping', 'contract', 'interim', 'consulting' but it's all hogwash because we're all temping now and that's about the size of it.

' *...but strongly feel I can make a real contribution to your plans for expansion.*' If you refer back here to the information you relayed in your first paragraph this helps to reinforce that you've done your homework and that this letter has been written just for them, which it has.

When making a direct approach never ask for an 'interview' because the person to whom you are writing, well, when they woke up that morning they weren't thinking of 'interviewing' anyone and that can scare the living daylights out of them. The word 'interview' implies that there is a defined vacancy for a specified person and a formal meeting must now be convened. No, in the great scheme of things people are much happier to have an informal meeting with you to 'discuss the possibilities' than they ever are to 'interview' you.

Now there is a school of thought, but not one to which I subscribe, which purports it to be a good idea for you to threaten to call them in a few days time to 'arrange a mutually convenient time for us to meet.' Well it's your call but as a reluctant networker this approach would be unlikely to sit well with you the seller and in my experience isn't well received by most buyers because they are much like you and resent this kind of hard-nosed approach. It can work well in a sales environment (and yes, you are of course *in* a sales environment) yet there is a certain, almost indefinable, dynamic between buyer and seller in this particular market that is not in your interests to interfere with.

So, on the balance of probability it's more likely that the 'pushy' ending would undo all the good work in your first two paragraphs. You may well want to give them a call a week or so later to confirm that they've received your letter and maybe fix a meeting so there's little point in threatening to do it.

Identifying Your Target Executive

So to whom do you write? Well, there's no 'silver bullet' answer to this as it will depend upon many variables, perhaps the type and size of the organization, the perceived level at which you might see yourself joining them or the type of problem they might want you to solve and not least the quality and type of information you have gleaned.

This may be an opportunity to let one or more of your troops know there's a war on if you feel they may be able to give you the inside track on this. It's unlikely that HR/Personnel will be the right target (unless of course that's the part of the organization you can solve a problem for) as they are typically the last people to know there's a need. Generalising here of course but in a large organization the HR function only get to know about the need when they are tasked to do something about it. By then it's nearly always too late because your letter will doubtless end up in their hands regardless of who you wrote to, and they will respond by inviting you to formally apply for the job when they advertise it in 2 weeks time.

Once a decision has been made to travel the costly and time consuming route of advertising or using an agency then that's exactly what they'll do, even if they've got the solution sitting in front of them for free. Anyway, that's one of the things HR people are hired to do and turkeys don't vote for Thanksgiving.

A smaller organization might be more flexible and meet you first to save some money for the company, but then a small organization is less likely to even have a dedicated HR team.

An observation I've made is that the Inverse Law of Cost Saving states that the larger the organization the less interested any one individual is in saving money for their employer.

Take care over inadvertently writing to gatekeepers. These may be the senior people in the part of the organization you would join who have the power to meet you but don't have the power to hire you. They have to defer to someone else, typically their boss. We saw earlier that one of the reasons needs arise is because of poor performers. *The gatekeeper may be that person* in which case your letter may not see the light of day.

One of the great truisms of the jobs market is that everyone wants to keep their job more than they want to give you one. Fear stalks the streets these days and everyone is in fear of losing their job. Everyone. So never write to a person that you believe might conceivably perceive you as a threat, because self-preservation sure does come to the fore. That gatekeeper may have a fancy job title but we know all about job titles. The chances are that they may have an old résumé/CV gathering dust in some bottom drawer but when they get your spanking new shiny state of the art fit for the 21st century résumé they'll reach for the smelling salts, even if in reality you're no threat to them at all. It's all perception.

You may be able to identify the decision maker. That's typically the one heading up that part of the organization you would join and who would have the power to hire you. Or in other words the person who will have the problem further down the track if they don't hire someone like you.

The general rule is that if you're in doubt travel first class and head straight for the top, not least because they haven't got where they are by being backwards in coming forwards and they often respect it when they see that quality in others. And that rule holds good even if you are at a fairly junior level - it can be a sign that you have potential and certainly initiative, a quality that all buyers want to buy. It's quite likely of course that the head honcho has a retinue of staff whose job it is to weed out all this stuff and act as a filter, and this is why and when the job begging letters get farmed out to the HR Department or by-pass them and go straight to re-cycling.

But if your letter is a bit more classy and businesslike then it stands a higher chance of getting through or at least filtering down the organization and finding its own level. Travelling down from the top does exert some psychological pressure on the recipient to do something about it. Anyway, if it trickles down and finds its way into the hands of the decision maker then that person may be mighty grateful to have found a replacement for that poorly performing gatekeeper who wouldn't have replied to you.

One bonus in travelling first class is that it's normally a lot easier to identify the more senior people in an organization than it ever is to find out the names of those lower down the food chain.

Getting Live Leads From Dead Ends

We already know that not everyone, or anyone, will want to buy everything, or anything, you are selling *at any given moment.* So logic and common sense tells us that, however good your information/intelligence, and however well written your direct approach, most of your direct approaches will fall on fallow ground.

Firstly, most 'job begging' letters don't get a response at all, maybe because the letter was so bad, maybe through ignorance and lack of empathy (which is a poor reflection on them) or maybe they simply don't have the time or resources to do so. A higher proportion of businesslike approaches do elicit a response, albeit negative. But let's look at the options:

No Response. How long should you wait for a response? Again, there's no silver bullet answer here but you've got the rest of your job search to get on with and much of what you do in your campaign will be driven, rightly, by your instincts.

As a general rule it doesn't pay to be passive when job hunting so if you've had no response at all review your approach and maybe give them a call after perhaps seven working days to confirm that they've received it. The hot time to make these calls is early morning or late afternoon as people are more receptive then than at other times when they are in meetings or fulfilling diary commitments. Persistence pays off so it might take you more than one attempt to get them to pick up. Did you inadvertently send it to someone who might see you as a threat? Send it again but this time to someone higher up the chain of command.

Taking 'no' for an answer is not an option when job hunting. For example, if you respond to a job advert for which you seemed to be the perfect match and get a 'rejection', or no reply at all, what are you going to do about it? Give them a call and ask them to look at it again. A lot of good candidates end up on the rejection pile by mistake. And don't be surprised if they tell you they never received your application. Pushing that 'send' button doesn't guarantee safe receipt. A lot of impressive CV's/résumés are still hovering around up there in the ether.

A Negative Response. This is not a 'rejection'. They are not saying 'we can't use you ever'. They can only be saying 'we can't use you *now*'. After all, it's unlikely that you will make a direct approach to an organization that could *never* use someone with your talents.

So the only thing you can get wrong with a good direct approach is the timing. What are you going to do about it? It's a real peculiarity of job-hunting that if a buyer declines to buy what we are trying to sell to them at the first attempt the seller is reluctant to approach them again *ever*. This is clearly a ludicrous 'mind-set' and one that doesn't exist in business. Imagine running your own business and not getting a sale from a potential customer 'Right, that's it. I've had it with you! It's over! Get outta here and don't come back!' Well, when you're running 'Job Search Inc' you can't afford to take that approach either so you might want to give your target executive a call, thank them for taking the trouble to respond, tell them you understand they don't have a current need but ask them if they know anyone who might have a need.

This is called 'getting live leads from dead ends' and a great example of networking someone you have never met or even known, and if you do it enough times it will restore your faith in human nature because on the whole people are kind and helpful.

Business people network with each other all the time and in a close knit industry, sector, or community they know what's going on. They are often privy to information not in the public domain and may well give you a lead, a name or advice if you ask for it. Getting live leads from dead ends in this way can be most productive.

Laying The Groundwork For A Second Approach

As a general rule once you've opened up a line of communication keep it open. If you've had a negative response write back to them. If you called them and they were helpful thank them for their time. If they gave you a lead tell them that you've done something about it. Then in your letter say something like...'As I *retain a strong interest in working with your company please do keep my résumé/CV on your file and perhaps you wouldn't mind if I contacted you again in the future'.*

Now that's a rhetorical question so you're not expecting a response and in effect the communication has ended. But it does make it easier for you to contact them at a later date. You now proceed with your campaign but if it grinds to a halt maybe two or three months down the track you can re-jig your CV / résumé a little and approach them again '...*You may recall our previous correspondence/discussion back in May at which point you were not in a position to hire. Having up-dated my résumé I'd be grateful if you could destroy the one on your file and replace it with this one. I would of course be very happy to meet with you informally if you would like to do so.*' Now two months is a long time in business just as it is in job hunting and needs may arise unexpectedly. You may now get a call from them asking you to come in and talk 'because things have moved on a bit'. In such ways do persistence and tenacity pay off. Incidentally, sending the 'up-dated' version of your résumé is helpful to them if they have not for some reason retained the original.

Getting A Positive Result

We know that most of your direct approaches will fall on fallow ground because the need to hire someone with your skills hasn't arisen. But there is a small 'window of time' within which your approach can land on their desk. This is the time so close to the need arising that your letter sparks their interest and fires up a phone call.

Now one thing that buyers can be fearful of is raising your expectations by making you believe that they have a specific role, clearly defined, and for which they would like to 'interview' you. This is rarely the case in this 'window' so they are more likely to *lower* your expectations by stating that they are not hiring but that they would still like you to come in for an informal discussion.

When you receive a telephone call from a stranger i.e. a new network acquaintance, your objective is not to get bogged down in a lengthy discussion over the phone but to clinch a face-to-face meeting. If the phone call goes on too long it's less likely that a meeting will take place because 'negatives' will intrude. Go with the flow but at the earliest appropriate opportunity get them to agree to a date for a meeting and then end the conversation. Follow up that conversation with an e-mail confirmation.

How you handle the meeting is not within the remit of this book and you might want to read 'Winning At Interview' for this. But for now, when you meet the buyer they should primarily be testing the ground, getting you to talk about yourself and figuring out whether you would fit in to their organization. There's nothing scientific about this and if they don't like you then the conversation is unlikely to go that far.

However, if after a period of time they start sharing with you quite specific information about their plans for the future and any needs that you could fulfil then that's a sign that a 'match' is being made. You're most unlikely to walk out of that meeting with anything close to an offer. But if the buyer is impressed it's likely that internal discussions will now take place and if they really see you as a quality person they may *create* a role for you or even hire you before they need you, because if they don't it will cost them time and money to find someone else as good as you in a few weeks or even months time.

Closing It All Down

When your campaign reaches a successful conclusion don't get so elated that you omit to tell your troops that the battle is won. If your troops come to you enthusiastically with some information only to discover that you started your new job a month ago then they won't be too enamoured with the idea of helping you out next time.

But also ensure that your elation at having secured an offer doesn't impel you to stand down your troops too soon and thus cut off the flow of information. It can be embarrassing if you have to go back to them should it unravel further down the track.

Give some thought to whom you might tell first and how you might tell them. It can be a bad tactic to think loosely about this so avoid the 'I'll tell her next time I see her' approach. It can be disrespectful for example for one of your key contacts to hear about your success via a third party.

This is all no more than common courtesy, but also remember that the shelf life of jobs is so short that you may have another battle to fight sooner than you think, and you will need to be in a position to hit the ground running.

It follows from that of course that all the documentation you have gathered together throughout your campaign, and there can be a lot of it, must be retained in readiness for your next battle.

---------♦ ♦ ♦ ---------

CONCLUSION

For all the reasons given in the previous Chapters, networking is a critical component of everyone's job search campaign, and that's something we all understand on an intellectual level, but because we don't do it regularly we're not that capable at it when we have to spring into '**Action**' at short notice.

Most 'reluctant' networkers therefore either don't do it at all or do it half-heartedly, with no real game plan. 'Enthusiastic' networkers go at it with great gusto but they don't have a game plan either and it all ends in tears. 'Network To Get Work' has given you a structure, which has served thousands of job hunters well - a sound strategy which will ensure that you maximise the flow of information that fuels your job search engine.

So line up your troops, get them in order, tell them there's a war on, send them the ammunition and have a brief and successful campaign. Oh - and incidentally, if you happen to have friends and acquaintances that may have an interest in reading 'Network To Get Work' do feel free to recommend it.

Alan Jones has been helping people to find the right jobs for 25 years. He is the author of several innovative, best selling books on job search and career building including 'Winning At Interview' and 'How To Negotiate Your Salary'.

'Winning At Interview' advocates a fresh and radical approach to the 'job interview' process. It demonstrates that with preparation and the right mental attitude you can win a job offer even when competing with more experienced and better qualified people.

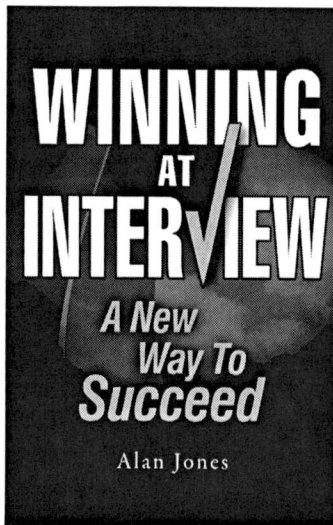

Have you ever taken a job at a lower salary than you might have achieved, if only you'd tried to negotiate a better deal? In 'How To Negotiate Your Salary' Alan Jones gives real insight into the process, and through 12 great Case Studies of some who failed and others who succeeded he helps to explore the issues, de-mystify the process and boost your confidence.

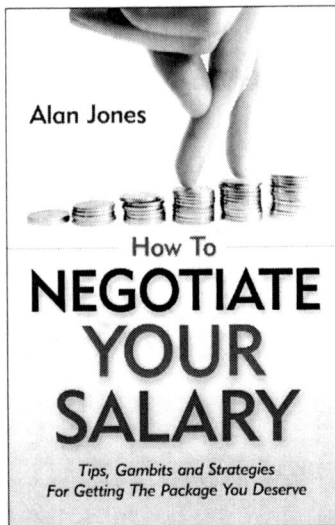

Alan Jones

How To
**NEGOTIATE
YOUR
SALARY**

*Tips, Gambits and Strategies
For Getting The Package You Deserve*

CPSIA information can be obtained at www.ICGtesting.com
Printed in the USA
LVOW13s1616280714

396371LV00001B/53/P